VOICES OF WAR

The Vietnam Conflict
War with Communism

Enzo George

Cavendish
Square
New York

Published in 2015 by Cavendish Square Publishing, LLC
243 5th Avenue, Suite 136, New York, NY 10016

© 2015 Brown Bear Books Ltd

First Edition

Website: cavendishsq.com

CPSIA Compliance Information: Batch #WS14CSQ

All websites were available and accurate when this book was sent to press.

Library of Congress Cataloging-in-Publication Data
George, Enzo.
The Vietnam Conflict : war with communism / Enzo George.
    pages cm. — (Voices of war)
Includes index.
ISBN 978-1-62712-873-5 (hardcover) ISBN 978-1-62712-875-9 (ebook)
1. Vietnam War, 1961-1975—Juvenile literature. I. Title.
DS557.7.S27 2014
959.704'3—dc23
                         2014008353

For Brown Bear Books Ltd:
Editorial Director: Lindsey Lowe
Managing Editor: Tim Cooke
Children's Publisher: Anne O'Daly
Design Manager: Keith Davis
Designer: Lynne Lennon
Picture Manager: Sophie Mortimer
Production Director: Alastair Gourlay

CONTENTS

Introduction

After World War II (1939–1945), the Vietnamese fought and defeated their French colonial rulers. North Vietnam became a communist country led by Ho Chi Minh. The United States was engaged in the Cold War, a global struggle for political influence with the communist Soviet Union. The U.S. government wanted to stop communism spreading. It sent military advisors to help South Vietnam resist attack by North Vietnam.

The North Vietnamese attacked a U.S. Navy ship in August 1964. The following year the first U.S. ground troops arrived in Vietnam. They were soon fighting the North Vietnamese Army (NVA) and the

A U.S. radioman calls for air support after a patrol comes under enemy fire in South Vietnam.

A transport helicopter flies in supplies to a U.S. forward artillery position.

Members of the National Guard clash with antiwar protestors at home. The war soon became unpopular in the United States.

Viet Cong, a communist guerrilla force based in South Vietnam. There were few battles. U.S. troops had to find and then try to destroy an elusive enemy that used ambush attacks before slipping away.

In January 1968 the communists launched the Tet Offensive. This huge attack was defeated but it convinced many Americans that the war could not be won. President Richard M. Nixon increasingly passed responsibility for the fighting to the South Vietnamese. The last U.S. soldiers left Vietnam in March 1973. Two years later, the North Vietnamese invaded and overthrew the South. Vietnam was finally reunified as a communist country.

The Road to War

After the French colonial government left Vietnam in 1953, war broke out between North and South Vietnam. The United States sent military support to the South in its fight against communism. When North Vietnam attacked U.S. ships in the Gulf of Tonkin on August 2, 1964, President Lyndon B. Johnson increased the U.S. military involvement. The Vietnam War was about to become an American conflict.

South Vietnamese soldiers practice firing their rifles. The United States provided advice and equipment to the Southern army.

French paratroopers land during the war against the Vietnamese. In 1953 the French decided to leave Vietnam.

❝ This new act of aggression, aimed directly at our own forces, again brings home to all of us in the United States the importance of the struggle for peace and security in Southeast Asia…

The determination of all Americans to carry out our full commitment to the people and to the government of South Vietnam will be redoubled by this outrage. Yet our response, for the present, will be limited and fitting. We Americans know, although others appear to forget, the risks of spreading conflict. We still seek no wider war… **❞**

President Lyndon B. Johnson addresses the American people about the Gulf of Tonkin incident on August 4, 1964.

GOING TO WAR FACTS

- The Vietnam War marked the height of the so-called Cold War, when the United States and the Soviet Union competed for political influence in the world.
- The "domino theory" suggested that if South Vietnam became communist, the rest of Southeast Asia would follow.
- The Vietnam War (1956–1975) was the longest war in U.S. history.
- It was the first modern war that the United States had lost.
- It was the most unpopular war in U.S. history and divided society.
- By the end of 1968, there were 536,000 American troops in Vietnam.

Recruitment and Training

Most U.S. troops in Vietnam were volunteers, but others were draftees who were forced to serve. Conscription had been used during World War II (1939–1945). In 1963 it was reintroduced by the Selective Service Act. Both volunteers and draftees were sent to training camps, or "boot camp," to learn how to be soldiers before being shipped out to join their units in Vietnam.

Recruits in Vietnam listen to a lecture about armaments during their acclimatization training.

❝ 'The Marine Corps Builds Men.' That was the recruiting slogan back then, and I wanted to be a man. More than that: I wanted to be a hero, and Marines were heroes almost by definition. The Halls of Montezuma. Belleau Wood. Guadalcanal. The Chosin Reservoir… Yes, indeed, if I was going, I was going as a Marine.

My parents were none too keen on the idea. It wasn't that they had any political or moral objections to the war, but only a question of who would want their child to go to war when he could go to college instead? But our long and sometimes heated discussions finally ended when I blurted out, 'Is this the way you raised me? To let other mothers' sons fight America's wars?' And of course, that was not the way my parents had raised me…

I left for boot camp at Parris Island, South Carolina, in June 1966, nine days after I graduated from high school. At the time, I did not even possess a draft card because, at 17, I was not yet old enough to register with Selective Service. **❞**

W.D. Ehrhart, 1st Battalion, 1st Marines, explains why he volunteered to serve.

RECRUITMENT FACTS

- 2.5 million U.S. soldiers served in Vietnam. Only around 20 percent saw combat. The rest served in support roles.
- Draftees made up about a quarter of the total number of recruits.
- The draft exempted college students and married men with children, which favored middle-class Americans.
- All recruits underwent an eight-week basic training course at boot camp and two weeks' acclimatization training when they arrived in Vietnam.
- Specialist training required a further eight to 26 weeks.
- The draft ended in 1973.

Weapons and Uniforms

The hot and humid Vietnamese climate caused many problems for standard-issue U.S. military uniforms and weapons. Soldiers found their cotton uniforms rotted in the damp air, their footwear was inadequate, and their rifles jammed. Both uniforms and weapons were improved over the course of the conflict. U.S. forces were issued flame throwers to burn away the thick vegetation and also sprayed Agent Orange, a poisonous chemical that stripped leaves from trees.

A U.S. soldier rests next to his M-60 machine gun. U.S. forces were better armed than the enemy.

" We would have our jungle fatigues [uniforms] on, which had side pouches on the hips for carrying… whatever you wanted to carry with you. You had your flak jacket, you would have your helmet, and of course your mosquito repellent, you would have your cartridge belt and in your cartridge belt you would have your first aid kit, your bayonet, and I would usually pack three or four grenades, the old M-26 grenades.

You would have your pack, and you wouldn't have everything in it because you're only going to go on a daytime patrol so in your pack (you'd) have extra ammunition, and you would have some C-rations because somewhere along there you're going to stop and have chow [food]. Then you would have, in my case at the time, an M-16 and I had three or four magazines [of bullets] loaded, and of course your water canteens. **"**

Mike Bradbury, K Company,
3rd Battalion, 26th Marines,
3rd Marine Division, describes
preparing to go on patrol.

A unit's helmets hang from their M-14 rifles early in the war. The M-14 was later replaced by the M-16.

EQUIPMENT FACTS

- Standard-issue cotton uniforms were gradually replaced with "Ripstop" nylon uniforms that were unpopular because they caused sweating.
- The waterproof rain poncho that soldiers carried doubled as a bedroll.
- Steel helmets were used to sit on and to carry valuables in order to protect them from the constant rain.
- Flamethrowers could shoot a flame a distance of 65 feet (20 m) and were used to destroy the dense foliage.
- Boots had reinforced soles to protect against the spikes the Viet Cong set as booby traps.

Living in Vietnam

Most soldiers served a 12-month "tour of duty" in Vietnam. Their living conditions depended on their rank. For the ordinary soldier, home was usually a tent. On patrol, all soldiers ate C-rations. These were complete packaged meals that provided 1,200 calories. Men had to wait until they were in a larger camp to get fresh food and purpose-built facilities such as washrooms and showers.

A U.S. soldier uses a bucket to wash at a U.S. camp in the Vietnamese jungle.

U.S. servicemen pay local people who have helped them to construct an army camp.

❝ Happy birthday to me… The officers fixed me an 'American' breakfast the next day. Instead of the usual cold rice and dried fish heads, they gave me cornflakes with chocolate milk!…

1st Cavalry moved in here a few weeks ago… They came here from the DMZ [demilitarized zone] and apparently these guys have been in the mud and the boonies [backwoods] for months… For the first twenty minutes or so, they just wandered around staring at everything, trying out all the chairs, flushing the toilets, etc. It was funny to watch. But I guess when you've had to do without clean clothes, good food, and shelter for as long as they have, you might not believe your eyes either. They kept saying they didn't believe anything like the club existed in Vietnam…

Last night we got a special treat. One of the officers brought back a movie projector. We showed an old John Wayne movie on a sheet stapled to the side of the building… It was weird to sit and watch an old WWII movie, surrounded by GIs, in a war zone! **❞**

Cathleen Cordova worked for Army Special Services, running U.S. clubs where soldiers came to relax after serving in the field.

LIFE IN VIETNAM FACTS

- Facilities at larger U.S. bases included purpose-built showers, movie screenings, television, and pool tables.
- Milk went bad quickly in the heat. Men drank cola or beer instead.
- Some soldiers bought fresh food directly from the Vietnamese.
- Soldiers spent a lot of time doing very little, so boredom was a big problem.
- Writing letters and receiving letters from home was the most popular pastime.
- Officers lived in purpose-built hut barracks.

International Allies

U.S. troops were part of an international effort to support South Vietnam. Soldiers from Australia, New Zealand, South Korea, and Canada also fought. Canada's official role in the war was to supply support to the United States, but many Canadians signed up for U.S. forces as volunteers. The Australian and New Zealand governments sent troops because they wanted U.S. support in the Pacific region.

South Korean soldiers on parade. Soldiers from South Korean had difficulty because they spoke a different language from their international allies.

" Then we went down there on another operation and one of my fellows tripped a mine… The immediate impact of that mine on the platoon was what is going on? Our fellows were being hurt and there was no one to take it out on. It's not a fair fight… From there it just got worse. The M16 mines then started to appear, and they were cutting a swathe through the company…

It got to the stage where it was a real effort to get the guys psyched up ready to move… I mean, guys would suddenly develop malaria and broken legs and all sorts of things. It had an enormous psychological impact on the men… It's all very well to say we'll take casualties in a minefield, but that is easy when it's not happening to you. You only need to have one guy wounded, slightly wounded, and it has an impact on everybody. "

Gordon Hurford commanded an infantry platoon of the 2 RAR (Royal Australian Regiment). Here he describes the psychological and physical trauma his soldiers faced on patrol.

ALLIES FACTS

- The South Koreans were the largest military presence after the Americans, with more than 300,000 troops.
- New Zealand's presence in Vietnam was extremely controversial and sparked antiwar protests across the country. Fewer than 4,000 troops served.
- Canada provided unofficial support to the United States.
- Although it was illegal for Canadians to join the U.S. armed forces, between 12,000 and 80,000 served in Vietnam.
- Australia sent around 60,000 personnel. They were in Vietnam from 1962 to 1972, Australia's longest-ever war.

Australian soldiers explore a Vietnamese village during a reconnaissance patrol.

The Enemy

A North Vietnamese gun crew scans the skies above Hanoi for enemy aicraft.

The official enemy in the war was North Vietnam, but it was backed by the Soviet Union and the People's Republic of China. The North Vietnamese Army (NVA) was well trained and equipped. North Vietnam also supported the Viet Cong, a huge guerrilla army in the South. The Viet Cong were not so well equipped, but still launched attacks on U.S. forces. The Americans were used to fighting large set-piece battles, but the war in Vietnam was fought in jungles and mountains with an enemy who was often hidden.

Ho Chi Minh was the leader of North Vietnam thoughout the war.

66 There must be one firm realization: guerrilla warfare is the base. Our resistance is an all-people resistance; that is the essential assurance for its final victory. Why do we call it an all-people resistance? All-people resistance means the entire people participate in the destruction of the invader. Carrying it one step further, all-people resistance also means that on the battlefield of the entire nation there are not only regular troops but also guerrillas… and there are self-defense militia participating in the fighting.

Therefore, to carry out all-people resistance, we must mobilize and arm the entire people. In order to cope with the war generally, and to cope with the enemy's new tactics, activating guerrilla warfare is all the more urgent…

If we develop guerrilla warfare, it will follow that, even though the enemy comes to a place which has no troops, they will still meet resistance, will at least be harassed, gradually worn down and destroyed one small bit at a time, so that our troops will have time to deal with them. 99

General Vo Nguyen Giap, the chief of staff in North Vietnam, planned the Vietnamese strategy against the United States.

NORTH VIETNAM FACTS

- The two largest communist states—China and the Soviet Union—supplied equipment, advisors, and funding to the North Vietnamese.
- Military aid and training turned the North Vietnamese Army (NVA) into a world-class force by the early 1960s.
- The United States aimed to fight a "limited" war to avoid conflict with either the Soviets or the Chinese.
- The communist strategy was to prolong the war until the U.S. government eventually made peace.
- North Vietnam involved all of its citizens in the fight against the South.

The South Vietnamese Army

This ARVN soldier has a grenade-launcher attached to his rifle.

The United States could not fight North Vietnam without support from the South Vietnamese people. The South Vietnamese drafted a new army, the Army of the Republic of Vietnam (ARVN). The ARVN was often seen by the international forces as an unreliable ally, although some observers rated them very highly. The men were thought to be badly disciplined, and their leaders corrupt. Late in the war, under a policy known as "Vietnamization," the ARVN were handed the responsibility for fighting by the Americans.

ARVN soldiers patrol through the jungle. Individual ARVN soldiers were often very brave and fought well alongside the Americans.

❝ U.S. soldiers are leaving, and you want the Vietnamese soldiers to take their place. But look at the U.S. soldier: he is well paid, well fed, well supported, gets good housing, doesn't have to worry about the safety of his wife and family while he's away, gets R&R trips and sometimes a trip home, and he can leave for good in one year.

The average ARVN soldier is not well-supported, makes very little money, and may live in squalor even when he is on leave, and knows he will be in the army for many years to come. Look at the soldiers' housing…pitiful. ❞

Captain Tram Buu was an ARVN interpreter. This is part of a conversation he had with a U.S. diplomat about the policy of Vietnamization.

SOUTH VIETNAMESE ARMY FACTS

- At its peak there were almost one million men serving in the ARVN, in either the Regular Army or in Regional or Popular Forces.
- The ARVN fought in every major battle of the Vietnam War.
- ARVN commanders were often accused of corruption and of being more interested in their own political advancement than military victory.
- 130,000 ARVN soldiers died during the war, and some 300,000 were wounded.

Jungle Warfare

The Vietnam War was fought in the dense jungles and mountains of South Vietnam. This suited the guerrilla tactics of the North Vietnamese much better than the tactics of the U.S. forces, whose armored vehicles and tanks were useless in the jungles. U.S. soldiers patrolled on foot in wet, humid conditions. Their uniforms rotted and their bodies were bitten by leeches. Constant rain and heat sapped their energy.

ARVN soldiers keep watch for the enemy in the jungle. The thick vegetation made it easy for the communists to launch ambushes.

> **"** The training was not as great as it should have been. It's what you learned once you got there. That's why the majority of people who got hurt or killed did it in the first couple of months….
>
> We worked out in the bush… You'd wear the same clothes and everything for thirty-five or forty days. That's why you'd get ringworm and jungle rot. The sores all over your body would break open and get all pussy and they wouldn't go away, especially in the monsoon season, when you were wet all the time….
>
> We couldn't really see the enemy because the jungle was so thick. We would fly around and try to draw their fire so that the Cobras [helicopters] would see the multiple flashes. I was beside the pilot. My job would be to return the fire and use smoke grenades to mark the positions where the fire was coming from…. **"**

Richard Malboeuf,
Canadian volunteer
serving in the U.S.
101st Airborne.

JUNGLE WARFARE FACTS

- To clear the dense foliage along the Ho Chi Minh Trail, the main communist supply route into South Vietnam, U.S. bombers dropped napalm and defoliation chemicals like Agent Orange.
- On the ground, soldiers used flamethrowers to destroy vegetation.
- Being unable to see the enemy had a profound psychological effect on U.S. soldiers on patrol.
- Heat, insects, and damp often harmed morale more than enemy action.
- The jungle was so thick, a path often had to be cut through it, leaving soldiers exposed to guerrilla attacks.

A soldier keeps his pack dry as a U.S. Army patrol crosses a river.

On Patrol

Soldiers crouch as a U.S. patrol tries to work out were a burst of enemy fire has come from.

As the war went on, U.S. commanders introduced a tactic named "search and destroy," in which patrols hunted for the enemy in the Vietnamese countryside. Foot patrols were the most hated part of a soldier's duty. The enemy laid mines and booby traps along routes they knew were often used by U.S. patrols. To stop this, U.S. commanders tried to alter their patrol routes every day.

U.S. soldiers look nervous as they cross a river. Fords were often booby-trapped by the enemy.

“ Every four nights (we) went out on night patrol. You never really followed the same pattern or trail or whatever. Each time you went out you'd deviate so that if they were watching you they wouldn't be able to ambush you in any one specific place at any specific time… One day you'd leave at ten o'clock and go out, then you'd shift to the south and the next day you might go out and shift to the north and then swing around and shift back to the south part way through your patrol…

It was amazing at night how much light there was over there because of the stars and the moon. During monsoon season, though, that was a totally different story. You could be out there in the monsoons and you couldn't see the guy a foot in front of you it rained so hard; it was just black. ”

Keith Erdman served with C Company, 1st Battalion, 4th Marine Regiment, 3rd Marine Division in Da Nang and along the Vietnamese border with Laos.

ON PATROL FACTS

- There were two main types of patrol: reconnaissance and "search and destroy."
- Reconnaissance patrols usually involved up to 100 men traveling short distances.
- Larger patrols carried out search-and-destroy missions to find and capture or kill the enemy.
- The most common enemy booby traps were punji stakes. These sharp bamboo spikes—often smeared with excrement—pierced soldiers' boots.
- Patroling was very tense. Fear of what might happen damaged morale.
- Infantry soldiers were taught during their training to trust no Vietnamese.

The Viet Cong

Young Viet Cong take shelter in a tiny underground bunker where they could also eat and sleep.

The Viet Cong were a tough enemy to fight. During the day they worked in the fields; at night they fought in small units, carrying out ambushes and guerrilla attacks. They were often poorly trained and lacked proper weapons but the constant threat they presented still terrified U.S. soldiers on patrol.

❝ The Viet Cong were small, quick, and carried nothing but a weapon, some ammunition, and a little dry rice. This kept them safe in battle, but it meant their day-to-day life was miserable. When they were hit, they had only herbal medicine to treat their wounds…

The government came after the Viet Cong with boats, planes, tanks, trucks, artillery, flamethrowers, and poisons, and still the Viet Cong fought back with what they had, which was mostly cleverness, terror, and the patience of the stones. When the Viet Cong could not be found (they spent most of their time, after all, hiding in caverns underground with entrances hidden by cook-stoves, bushes, false floors, or even underwater by flowing rivers themselves), the Republican soldiers took out their frustration on us: arresting nearby farmers and beating or shooting them on the spot, or carting anyone who looked suspicious off to jail. ❞

Le Ly Hayslip was a peasant girl who worked with the Viet Cong near Da Nang for three years.

VIET CONG FACTS

- The official name of the Viet Cong was the National Liberation Front (NLF).
- The Viet Cong's role was to carry out attacks in South Vietnam in support of the North Vietnamese Army.
- By 1968 there were as many as 400,000 Viet Cong operating in South Vietnam.
- The Viet Cong lived with villagers and also in underground tunnels.
- By 1965 the Viet Cong controlled nearly sixty percent of the countryside in South Vietnam.

Viet Cong fighters use boats to travel along a river in South Vietnam.

The Bombing War

A U.S. B-52 bomber drops bombs above North Vietnam. The Vietnamese had no defenses against the bombers.

The air power of the U.S. forces was greatly superior to that of the enemy. Early in the war President Lyndon B. Johnson ordered Operation Rolling Thunder. This bombing campaign against targets in North Vietnam lasted from 1965 to 1968. Despite suffering great damage, the North Vietnamese withstood the attack. A second U.S. bombing campaign was ordered by President Richard M. Nixon in 1972. It finally forced North Vietnam to begin peace talks.

A U.S. ground crew loads a bomb beneath the wing of a Super Sabre F-100D jet.

66 Slightly after midnight, I am sitting in the cockpit of my airplane. It is a jet fighter, a Phantom… We are off… Soon I make radio contact with another craft, a big one, a gunship, painted black and flying very low…

I am there to keep enemy guns off him and to help him kill trucks. Funny, he can see the trucks but not the guns 'til they're on him. I cannot see the trucks but pick the guns up as soon as the first rounds flash out on the muzzles.

Sometimes, when I drop, pass after pass, great fire balls will roll and boil upwards; and a large, rectangular fire will let us know we've hit another supply truck. Then we will probe with firepower all around that truck to find if there are more. Often we will touch off several, their fires outlining the trail or truck park. 99

Major Mark E. Berent, 8th Tactical Fighter Wing, on attacking the Ho Chi Minh Trail, the main supply route into South Vietnam.

BOMBING FACTS

- Operation Rolling Thunder started on March 2, 1965. It continued until November 2, 1968. Its aim was to bring North Vietnam to the negotiating table. It failed, despite U.S. pilots dropping 643,000 tons of bombs.
- Operation Ranch Hand was an aerial campaign to spray nineteen million gallons of herbicide across six million acres of Southeast Asia between 1962 and 1971.
- Operation Linebacker II was an 11-day campaign in December 1972 in which U.S. bombers flew 2,123 missions, mostly at night.

The Helicopter War

First used in the Korean War (1950–1953), helicopters became vital in Vietnam. They were the best means of moving troops and equipment in the jungles. They could transport troops to remote locations and evacuate wounded soldiers rapidly. The Chinook was used for heavy transportation; the Cobra was a gunship; but the most common "chopper" was the Bell UH-1 Iroquois, or "Huey."

A helicopter gunner keeps a look out for the enemy as a UH-1D Huey evacuates U.S. soldiers after a patrol.

A Navy airman onboard a UH-1B Huey fires his twin machine guns at targets in the Mekong Delta.

66 This particular night there was no moon and it was like flying in a barrel with the lid on. It was so black you could not even see the jungle far below… The mission—extract a team that was in trouble…

As we neared the LZ [landing zone] it was obvious we were in for a big challenge. It was covered in elephant grass, that is grass that is 10-12 feet [3–3.5 m] tall, and the gunships had set it on fire, and it was now a raging fire as we approached. As I descended into the LZ to pick up the waiting troops it was immediately apparent we were potentially in grave danger…

As the helicopter approached the tree line the team was hiding. In they came on the run as the gunships continued their gun runs… As we lifted off, we were now surrounded on three sides with flames… 99

Don Douglas, combat helicopter pilot, 117th Assault Helicopter Company, 1969.

HELICOPTER WAR FACTS

- Helicopters could take off and land in small spaces, making them ideal for Vietnam, where there were few roads.
- The UH-I Iroquois was better known by its nickname of "Huey."
- The Huey's jobs included inserting troops into hostile territory and rescuing more than 500,000 wounded soldiers.
- The AH-1 Cobra was a gunship that carried out short-range, low-level strikes against enemy targets.
- The Chinook could cary up to fourteen fully-equipped combat troops.
- Of the 12,000 helicopters used in Vietnam, 4,869 were lost.

Tunnel Warfare

Ronald Headly, a Tunnel Rat from 65th Engineer Battalion, checks the entrance of a Viet Cong tunnel.

The Viet Cong were an elusive enemy. Using basic tools they dug out networks of tunnels to hide from the Americans. At Cu Chi they dug over 100 miles (160 km) of tunnels to connect local villages. The underground complex had a hospital, kitchens, sleeping quarters, and armament factories. The "Tunnel Rats" were U.S. soldiers who entered the underground networks to fight the enemy.

" You had to control and direct the fear. You made each movement with infinite care. Your senses never were more acute… We'd enter the tunnel one at a time, separated by several feet, so a grenade wouldn't get us all. You'd feel your way along for booby traps. It got so you could sense them. The same for VC [Viet Cong]. You could smell another human being in the tunnel. You knew he was waiting for you in the dark…

The VC would take a snake: we used to call them 'one-step' or 'two-step' snakes. They were bamboo vipers and once bitten, you could only take one or two more steps before you died. Charlie [the Viet Cong] would tie the viper in a piece of bamboo with a piece of string. As the Tunnel Rat went through, he'd knock it, and the snake would come out and bite him in the neck or face… We also met hornets, centipedes, great moving masses of black spiders, bats. We met rats that carried bubonic plague. "

Jack Flowers, Tunnel Rat Unit, 1st Infantry Division, entered 97 enemy tunnels in Vietnam.

TUNNEL WARFARE FACTS

- Tunnels were extremely well disguised. One network was so well hidden the U.S. 25th Division built its base camp on top.
- Some tunnels were up to 23 feet (7m) below the ground.
- The largest complexes could house as many as 16,000 Viet Cong, who could live underground for months at a time.
- The "Tunnel Rats" were all volunteers from the U.S., Australian, or New Zealand infantry.
- They entered the tunnels with little more than a flashlight and a pistol.
- Once cleared, tunnels were blown up with explosive charges.

Tunnel Rat Ronald Payne explores a tunnel armed with only his flashlight and a Colt 1911 pistol.

Under Siege at Khe Sanh

The U.S. Marine combat base at Khe Sanh was in a remote region in the northwest corner of South Vietnam. It lay near the Ho Chi Minh Trail, the communist supply line from North Vietnam to the south. In January 1968 some 40,000 North Vietnamese surrounded the 6,000 Marines at Khe Sanh. Despite the heavy odds against them, the Marines held out for 77 days.

Smoke billows from U.S. airstrikes on North Vietnamese positions outside the perimeter at Khe Sanh.

A view from a U.S. helicopter shows the remote base at Khe Sanh far below.

“ Throughout late February and March, the NVA [North Vietnamese Army] answered the air bombardment with daily barrages from artillery dug into the hills surrounding the base. On some days the base would receive a thousand rounds or more, with an average of two thousand five hundred rounds per week. Morale remained miraculously high, however, considering the circumstances…

My worst experience came on the evening of March 22, 1968. It had been rumored for weeks that the NVA would launch a ground assault against the base to coincide with the anniversary of the March 1954 assault on the French stronghold at Dien Bien Phu. At about 2100 hours the NVA began an intense artillery, rocket, and mortar barrage. The concentration of incoming artillery and mortar rounds was the heaviest I had ever experienced, and we feared that the NVA would launch a ground assault under the cover of this barrage. **”**

Platoon leader Bruce M. Geiger was in charge of eight light tanks during the siege of Khe Sanh.

KHE SANH FACTS

- The siege of Khe Sanh began on January 20, 1968 and lasted until April 8, 1968.
- U.S. fighter-bombers and B-52s bombed the NVA positions round the clock.
- In the most concentrated bombing in history, U.S. aircraft dropped the equivalent bomb tonnage of ten Hiroshima atomic bombs.
- Ground units arrived on April 8 to relieve the Marines, ending the siege.
- U.S. and ARVN losses stood at 400; NVA losses were around 12,000.
- The Marines' stand at Khe Sanh was a welcome morale boost for U.S. forces and their allies.

The Tet Offensive

The New Year holiday, or Tet, was usually marked by a ceasefire. But on the morning of Tet on January 30, 1968, more than 84,000 Viet Cong and NVA troops attacked more than 40 towns and cities in South Vietnam. The initial attacks were successful. In Saigon, fighters even entered the U.S. Embassy compound. The offensive was defeated, but it was a huge blow for U.S. forces and increased the growing opposition to the war at home.

U.S. Marines in Hue climb a mound of rubble as they fight their way into the ancient Citadel in February 1968.

ARVN Rangers take cover at the side of a road as they defend Saigon from the communist offensive.

❝ Well as morning arrived we soon realized that there were a lot of NVA troops all around the hotel. It appeared they just drove in and took over the town. They had to know we were in the hotel because our truck was parked outside in plain sight…

Word was spreading fast that something big had happened and we were not the only place under attack… Since the enemy was not showing any interest in trying to take us on we were asked not to start a firefight. So we did what we did a lot of in the Army, we sat around and waited and watched…

I for one could not remember the last time I even fired my weapon… Well the order came and I fired my first shot at a real live person. Not surprising, I missed. I hit the wall of the building he was standing next to. I only missed by a few inches but that gave him time to bring his rifle up and point it in my direction. My next shot did not miss, and I was relieved that he did not get a shot off… ❞

Warren "Skip" Galinski, Army Security Agency (ASA), was staying in the resort town of Dalat when the Tet Offensive started.

TET OFFENSIVE FACTS

- During the Vietnam War, Tet was usually marked by a temporary ceasefire.
- Fighting in Saigon lasted until February 24, 1968, when the ARVN and U.S. troops finally won back the city.
- Americans at home watched live television pictures of the storming of the U.S. Embassy.
- Communist forces took over the old imperial capital of Hue and resisted intense U.S. attacks until March 3.
- The NVA and Viet Cong lost 15,000 fighters killed and 20,000 wounded, but pressed on with the siege of the U.S. Marine firebase at Khe Sanh.

Protest on the Home Front

The Vietnam War divided U.S. society. Most Americans originally supported the conflict but an anti-war movement developed in the late 1960s. Protests spread from small demonstrations on university campuses to large-scale marches in major cities. The protestors objected to the war being fought at all, but also to what they saw as an unfair draft system.

An African-American protest on Fifth Avenue, New York City, calls for black troops to be brought home.

Opponents of the war protest outside the White House in Washington, D.C., in November 1969.

66 It was routine during the two weeks [in the Pentagon] when the Vietnam War was going on, for the protestors to be waiting on the steps of the Pentagon every morning and usually they would have some kind of crazy uniform on or a skeleton… You would step over them in order to get into the front door. And at one point, someone had put a bomb in one of the men's latrines, which exploded and probably did a lot of damage, but it didn't hurt anybody…

(The demonstrators) tried to be there as everybody entered. They'd try to insult you… I never did hear anybody argue with them or try to even reply. The best thing to do is to ignore them… But as far as I ever observed, they never tried to block, they just tried to insult… 99

Seldon Graham was a Korean War veteran and an Army reservist. During the Vietnam War he worked in the Pentagon in Washington, D.C., for two weeks each year.

HOME FRONT FACTS

- Two-thirds of Americans supported the war in the summer of 1965.
- Burning a draft card became a federal offense in mid-October 1965.
- President Nixon's expansion of the war led to 250,000 people marching on Washington, D.C., on October 15, 1969.
- By 1967, the country was deeply divided over the war.
- On May 4, 1970, the National Guard opened fire on an antiwar protest at Kent State University, Ohio, killing four students.
- By April 1971, seventy-three percent of Americans wanted the war to end.

Medicine and Nursing

The treatment of wounded soldiers improved dramatically during the Vietnam War thanks to the introduction of "medevac,' or medical evacuation. Helicopters took casualties directly from the battlefield to an operating table in a field hospital within one hour. This saved the lives of many soldiers. Medics also accompanied patrols so that they could treat injured soldiers. Helicopters were stationed around the country ready to react to radio calls for medical evacuation.

Casualties on stretchers wait to be examined by doctors on the deck of one of the two U.S. Navy hospital ships stationed in Vietnam.

Army medics perform emergency first aid on a soldier wounded on patrol.

MEDICINE FACTS

- In 1965 there were just two U.S. military hospitals in Vietnam. By 1969 there were thirty hospitals and 5,000 beds.
- In World War II, one in three injured soldiers died from his wounds. In Vietnam, this had fallen to one in five.
- Helicopters were a vital part of the medevac procedure. If a helicopter could not land or came under fire, injured soldiers were picked up on litters lowered on steel cables.
- About 16,000 U.S. doctors and 15,000 nurses served in Vietnam.
- Poor hygiene and insect bites caused many illnesses.

66 The reality of the combat zone hit me the minute our plane landed in. It was getting dark and there were two guards out on the tarmac. They said 'nurses out first,' and on the steps down, I saw the guards wore bandoliers [ammunition belts] and carried huge weapons. It wasn't the 6 o'clock news…

I got reassigned to the 71st Evacuation Hospital in Pleiku. We were close to the Cambodian border and we got casualties directly from the field. We tried to stabilize them, treat their shock, stop their bleeding, get the chest tubes in, do the tracheostomy, do the triage, get the IV in and all the frontline stuff. We would have to make the decision if they were going to be shipped home or sent back out. It was hard sending people back. 99

Diane Carlson Evans enlisted in the U.S. Army after she had finished her nursing studies, aged 21.

Recreation and Entertainment

The United Services Organization (USO) organized entertainment for troops in Vietnam. Hollywood stars and professional football players flew to the war zone. Troops also relaxed at USO clubs. Music was popular, particularly one hit song from the charts back home, "We Gotta Get out of this Place" by the 1960s' English band The Animals.

A huge audience of service personnel wait at Long Binh for an appearance by the entertainer Bob Hope on Christmas Day 1971.

U.S. soldiers write letters home outside their improvised living quarters.

66 They had quite a convoy accompanying us [to the base]. There were five jeeps and two large trucks. Each jeep had a driver and a machine gun mounted on the front for the number two man to operate. The third man carried a mobile radio and was armed as well. The fourth passenger was one Hilltop Singer in complete camouflage including netting covering our faces… When I asked why we were being taken up in separate jeeps, it was explained to me that if we came under fire there was a better chance of the show going on, maybe as a duet, but that most of us would make it that way…

Anyhow, when we got there and climbed out of those fatigues [pants] into our miniskirts, hose and heels, it was quite a treat to our countrymen. The show was well received, and we feel we did a great job in boosting the morale at that location. 99

Linda was one of the Hilltop Singers, a singing trio who visited Vietnam in 1971 and 1972 to entertain U.S. troops.

ENTERTAINMENT FACTS

- At the peak of operations, seventeen USO clubs entertained more than one million service personnel in Vietnam every month.
- The USO slogan was "home away from home."
- USO clubs had a store, barber, telephone, and hot showers.
- Soldiers earned two weeks' leave after six months' active duty.
- Bob Hope, Ann Margaret, Raquel Welch, and John Wayne were among the stars who performed live for the troops.
- Because letters were so important, mail was delivered daily by helicopter.

Keeping Up Morale

Early in the war the spirits of the troops were generally high, but by the late 1960s they had fallen. Later, as it became clear that U.S. military objectives would never be met, morale fell further. Many soldiers alternated between fear and boredom, both of which were bad for morale. When the troops learned how unpopular the war was back home in the United States, morale fell even further.

U.S. soldiers read comic books to pass the time. Boredom was a great problem for many troops.

Weary U.S. soldiers take a break during a jungle patrol. Such patrols greatly damaged morale.

> My own doubts about the war began to surface that summer. As the weeks wore on and I spent more time in the field witnessing the casualties, the pursuit of this war became more and more depressing. I began to realize the futility of fighting a guerrilla war with massive firepower and trying to decimate NVA battalions that kept replenishing themselves from a seemingly endless supply of manpower.
>
> American soldiers were battling for possession of the same hill again and again, hill after hill, sacrificing so many lives for worthless terrain. Despite my loathing of communism and my belief that we could not walk away from the South Vietnamese who had asked for our help, I too began to feel the war was a terrible mistake, a sacrifice too great for any country, including my own, to bear.

Journalist Jurate Kazickas was one of just 70 female reporters to cover the war in Vietnam. Here she recalls her feelings about the war in the summer of 1967.

MORALE FACTS

- The unconventional nature of the war—the booby traps, guerrilla fighting, foot patrols, and jungle conditions—all sapped morale.
- The United States was still a segregated society, and racial tensions in the military added to the loss of morale.
- A lack of morale led to a lack of discipline and increased incidents of fragging. Fragging was when soldiers intentionally wounded or killed their own officers. Incidents of fragging grew as morale fell. In 1969, there were 126 cases; in 1971, there were 333, including 12 deaths.

The End of the War

An NVA tank breaks through the gates of the presidential palace in Saigon on April 30, 1975.

Richard M. Nixon was elected U.S. president in 1968 on a promise of ending the war. He began a program of Vietnamization. The ARVN increasingly took over the fighting, allowing U.S. troops to leave. The last U.S. troops left Vietnam in March 1973. Two years later, the NVA launched a final attack on Saigon. They captured the city and reunified Vietnam as a communist state.

Young Americans wait at a naval air station to welcome home U.S. prisoners of war returning from Vietnam in March 1973.

" I don't know who will get home first, me or this letter… I got a call through to my parents a little while after I talked to you. My mother did not believe that I was coming home. But I finally got through to her. And, boy, was she happy…

You don't know how close I have been to getting killed or maimed. Too many times I have seen guys near me get hit and go home in a plastic bag. Like I have said before, someone was looking over me. Well, it is all over now. Now it's time to forget. But it's hard to forget these things. I close my eyes and try to sleep, but all I can see is Jenkins lying there with his brains hanging out or Lefty with his eyes shot out…. Then you stop to think it could be me. Hell, I don't know why I am writing all this. But it feels better getting it out of my mind. "

Peter H. Roepcke was an infantryman with A Company, 3rd Battalion, 506th Infantry, 101st Airborne Division. He wrote this letter to his girlfriend, Gail, to tell her he was coming home.

END OF THE WAR FACTS

- The ARVN had almost a million men; the United States supplied their former allies with the latest weapons.
- The communists had just 150,000 troops in South Vietnam.
- The communists spent two years building up their forces, before attacking and defeating the South in 1975.
- American casualties in Vietnam were 58,000 dead and more than 300,000 wounded. ARVN casualties were 130,000 dead and 500,000 injured.
- The NVA and Viet Cong lost a total of about a million civilian and military dead and about 600,000 wounded.

GLOSSARY

acclimatization A period of getting used to new surroundings.

ambush A surprise attack by attackers who have been lying in wait.

bandolier A shoulder belt that has hoops to carry ammunition.

chief of staff The senior military commander in an army.

colonial Relating to a land governed by another country.

conscription Compulsory recruitment into the armed services.

defoliation Stripping leaves from trees and bushes.

draft The system of selecting citizens for compulsory military service.

field hospital A temporary hospital set up near a battlefield to deal with casualties.

guerrilla A soldier who fights by unconventional means, such as ambush, sabotage, or terrorism.

gunship A heavily armed helicopter.

litter A basic type of stretcher.

medevac The evacuation of wounded casualties by helicopter or aircraft.

morale How positive or negative a person or group feels about achieving a particular task.

napalm A flammable jelly that was used in bombs to start fires.

propaganda Information that is intended to encourage support for one side in a struggle, or to damage support for the other side.

reconnaissance The observation of a region in order to find out about the location of the enemy.

tour of duty The length of time a military person spends on active duty.

Vietnamization The policy of withdrawing U.S. soldiers from Vietnam and leaving the fighting to the South Vietnamese.

FURTHER INFORMATION

Books

Benoit, Peter. *The Vietnam War* (Cornerstones of Freedom). Children's Press, 2013.

Gitlin, Martin. *U.S. Involvement in Vietnam* (Essential Events). Abdo Publishing Company, 2010.

Mason, Andrew. *The Vietnam War: A Primary Source History* (In Their Own Words). Gareth Stevens Publishing, 2005.

Perritano, John. *Vietnam War* (America at War). Scholastic, 2010.

Senker, Cath. *The Vietnam War* (Living Through). Heinemann-Raintree, 2012.

Tougas, Shelley. *Weapons, Gear, and Uniforms of the Vietnam War* (Equipped for Battle). Capstone Press, 2012.

Websites

http://www.eyewitnesstohistory.com/cwfrm.htm
Links to numerous first-hand accounts from Eyewitness to History.

http://www.history.com/topics/vietnam-war
History.com guide with links to many articles about the war.

http://www.pbs.org/wgbh/amex/vietnam/
PBS site to accompany the series *Vietnam: A Television History*.

http://www.historyplace.com/unitedstates/vietnam/
The History Place page, with timelines for the whole conflict.

Publisher's note to educators and parents: Our editors have carefully reviewed these websites to ensure that they are suitable for students. Many websites change frequently, however, and we cannot guarantee that a site's future contents will continue to meet our high standards of quality and educational value. Be advised that students should be closely supervised whenever they access the Internet.

INDEX